IN PALESTINE

AND OTHER POEMS

By R. W. Gilder.

♧

THE NEW DAY
THE CELESTIAL PASSION
LYRICS
TWO WORLDS
THE GREAT REMEMBRANCE
THE ABOVE ALSO IN ONE VOLUME ENTITLED
FIVE BOOKS OF SONG
A SELECTION ENTITLED
"FOR THE COUNTRY"
IN PALESTINE AND OTHER POEMS

IN PALESTINE

AND OTHER POEMS

BY

RICHARD WATSON GILDER

NEW YORK
THE CENTURY CO.

THE DE VINNE PRESS.

CONTENTS.

I

II

III

IV

I

IN PALESTINE.

AH no! that sacred land
Where fell the wearied feet of the lone Christ
Robs not the soul of faith. I shall set down
The thought was in my heart. If that hath lost
Aught of its child-belief, 't was long ago,
Not there in Palestine; and if 't were lost,
He were a coward who should fear to lose
A blind, hereditary, thoughtless faith,—
Comfort of fearful minds, a straw to catch at
On the deep-gulfed and tempest-driven sea.

Full well I know how shallow spirits lack
The essence, flinging from them but the form;
I have seen souls lead barren lives and cursed,—
Bereft of light, and all the grace of life,—
Because for them the inner truth was lost
In the frail symbol—hated, shattered, spurned.

But faith that lives forever is not bound
To any outward semblance, any scheme
Fine-wrought of human wonder, or self-love,
Or the base fear of never-ending pain.
True faith doth face the blackness of despair,—
Blank faithlessness itself; bravely it holds
To duty unrewarded and unshared;
It loves where all is loveless; it endures
In the long passion of the soul for God.

'T was thus I thought:—
At last the very land whose breath he breathed,
The very hills his bruisèd feet did climb!
This is his Olivet; on this Mount he stood,
As I do now, and with this same surprise
Straight down into the startling blue he gazed
Of the fair, turquoise mid-sea of the plain.
That long, straight, misty, dream-like, violet wall
Of Moab,—lo, how close it looms; the same
Quick human wonder struck his holy vision.
About these feet the flowers he knew so well.
Back where the city's shadow slowly climbs

There is a wood of olives gaunt and gray,
And centuries old; it holds the name it bore
That night of agony and bloody sweat.

I tell you when I looked upon these fields
And stony valleys,—through the purple veil
Of twilight, or what time the Orient sun
Made shining jewels of the barren rocks,—
Something within me trembled; for I said:
This picture once was mirrored in his eyes;
This sky, that lake, those hills, this loveliness,
To him familiar were; this is the way
To Bethany; the red anemones
Along yon wandering path mark the steep road
To green-embowered Jordan. All is his:
These leprous outcasts pleading piteously;
This troubled country,—troubled then as now,
And wild and bloody,—this is his own land.
On such a day, girdled by these same hills,
Pressed by this dark-browed, sullen, Orient crowd,
On yonder mount, spotted with crimson blooms,
He closed his eyes, in that dark tragedy

Which mortal spirit never dared to sound.
O God! I saw those haunting eyes in every
throng.

Were he divine, and maker of all worlds,—
The Godhead veiled in suffering, for our sins,—
An unimagined splendor poured on earth
In sacrifice supreme,—this were a scene
Fit for the tears of angels and all men.
If he were man,—a passionate human heart,
Like unto ours, but with intenser fire,
And whiter from the deep and central glow;
Who loved all men as never man before,
Who felt as never mortal all the weight
Of this world's sorrow, and whose hand
Upstretched in prayer did seem, indeed, to clutch
The hand divine; if he were man, yet dreamed
That the Ineffable through him had power—
Even through his touch—to scatter human pain
(Setting the eternal seal on his high hope
And promised kingdom); were he only man,
Thus, thus to aspire, and thus at last to fall!

Such anguish! such betrayal! Who could paint
That tragedy! one human, piteous cry—
"Forsaken!"—and black death! If he were God,
'T was for an instant only, his despair;
Or were he man, and there is life beyond,
And, soon or late, the good rewarded are,
Then, too, is recompense.

But were he man,
And death ends all; then was that tortured death
On Calvary a thing to make the pulse
Of memory quail and stop.

The blackest thought
The human brain may harbor comes that way.
Face that,—face all,—yet lose not hope nor
heart!
One perfect moment in the life of love,
One deed wherein the soul unselfed gleams forth,—
These can outmatch all ill, all doubt, all fear,
And through the encompassing burden of the world
Burn swift the spirit's pathway to its God.

THE ANGER OF CHRIST.

I.

ON the day that Christ ascended
To Jerusalem,
Singing multitudes attended,
And the very heavens were rended
With the shout of them.

II.

Chanted they a sacred ditty,
Every heart elate;
But he wept in brooding pity,
Then went in the holy city
By the Golden Gate.

III.

In the temple, lo! what lightning
Makes unseemly rout!
He in anger, sudden, frightening,
Drives with scorn and scourge the whitening
Money-changers out.

IV.

By the way that Christ descended
From Mount Olivet,
I, a lonely pilgrim, wended,
On the day his entry splendid
Is remembered yet.

V.

And I thought: If he, returning
On this festival,
Here should haste with love and yearning,
Where would now his fearful, burning
Anger flash and fall?

VI.

In the very house they builded
            To his saving name,
'Mid their altars, gemmed and gilded,
Would his scourge and scorn be wielded,
            His fierce lightning flame.

VII.

Once again, O Man of Wonder,
            Let thy voice be heard!
Speak as with a sound of thunder;
Drive the false thy roof from under;
            Teach thy priests thy word.

THE BIRDS OF BETHLEHEM.

I.

I HEARD the bells of Bethlehem ring—
  Their voice was sweeter than the priests';
I heard the birds of Bethlehem sing
  Unbidden in the churchly feasts.

II.

They clung and sung on the swinging chain
  High in the dim and incensed air;
The priests, with repetitions vain,
  Chanted a never-ending prayer.

III.

So bell and bird and priest I heard,
  But voice of bird was most to me;
It had no ritual, no word,
  And yet it sounded true and free.

IV.

I thought Child Jesus, were he there,
  Would like the singing birds the best,
And clutch his little hands in air
  And smile upon his mother's breast.

Bethlehem, Holy Week, 1896.

NOËL.

I.

STAR-DUST and vaporous light,—
  The mist of worlds unborn,—
A shuddering in the awful night
  Of winds that bring the morn.

II.

Now comes the dawn: the circling earth;
  Creatures that fly and crawl;
And Man, that last, imperial birth;
  And Christ, the flower of all.

"THE SUPPER AT EMMAUS."

(A PICTURE BY REMBRANDT.)

WISE Rembrandt! thou couldst paint, and thou alone,
Eyes that had seen what never human eyes
Before had looked on; him that late had passed
Onward and back through gates of Death and Life.

O human face where the celestial gleam
Lingers! Oh, still to thee the eyes of men
Turn with deep, questioning worship; seeing there,
As in a mirror, the Eternal Light
Caught from the shining of the central Soul
Whence came all worlds, and whither shall return.

THE DOUBTER.

I.

Thou Christ, my soul is hurt and bruised!
With words the scholars wear me out;
My brain o'erwearied and confused,—
Thee, and myself, and all I doubt.

II.

And must I back to darkness go
Because I cannot say their creed?
I know not what I think; I know
Only that thou art what I need.

THE PARTHENON BY MOONLIGHT.

I.

THIS is an island of the golden Past
  Uplifted in the tranquil sea of night.
In the white splendor how the heart beats fast,
  When climbs the pilgrim to this gleaming height;—
As might a soul, new-born, its wondering way
  Take through the gates of pearl and up the stair
Into the precincts of celestial day,—
  So to this shrine my worshiping feet did fare.

II.

But look! what tragic waste! Is Time so lavish
  Of dear perfection thus to see it spilled?
'T was worth an empire;—now behold the ravish
  That laid it low. The soaring plain is filled

With the wide-scattered letters of one word
  Of loveliness that nevermore was spoken;
Nor ever shall its like again be heard:
  Not dead is art—but that high charm is broken.

III.

Now moonlight builds with swift and mystic art
  And makes the ruin whole—and yet not whole;
But exquisite, though crushed and torn apart.
  Back to the temple steals its living soul
In the star-silent night; it comes all pale,—
  A spirit breathing beauty and delight,—
And yet how stricken! Hark! I hear it wail
  Self-sorrowful, while every wound bleeds white.

IV.

And though more sad than is the nightingale
  That mourns in Lykabettos' fragrant pine,
That soul to mine brings solace; nor shall fail
  To heal the heart of man while still doth shine

Yon planet, doubly bright in this deep blue;
  Yon moon that brims with fire these violet hills:
For beauty is of God; and God is true,
  And with his strength the soul of mortal fills.

THE OTTOMAN EMPIRE.

I.

LET fall the ruin propped by Europe's hands!
  Its tottering walls are but a nest of crime;
Slayers and ravishers in licensed bands
  Swarm darkly forth to shame the face of Time.

II.

False, imbecile, and cruel; kept in place
  Not by its natural force, but by the fears
Of foes, scared each of each; even by the grace
  Of rivals—not blood-guiltless all these years!

III.

Aye, let the ruin fall, and from its stones
  Rebuild a civic temple pure and fair,
Where freedom is not alien; where the groans
  Of dying and ravished burden not the air!

1896.

KARNAK.

I.

Of all earth's shrines this is the mightiest,
  And none is elder. Pylon, obelisk,
Column enormous,—seek or east or west,
  No temple like to Karnak 'neath the disk
Of the far-searching sun. Since the first stone
  Here lifted to the heavens its dumb appeal,
Empires and races to the dread unknown
  Have passed,—gods great and small 'neath Time's slow wheel
Have fallen and been crushed;—the earth hath shaken
Ruin on ruin—desolate, dead, forsaken.

II.

Since first these stones were laid, the solid world,
  Aye, this whole, visible, infinite universe,
Hath shifted on its base; suns have been hurled
  From heaven; the ever-circling spheres rehearse
A music new to men. Yet still doth run
  This river, throbbing life through all its lands;
Those desert mountains lifted to the sun
  Live as of old; and these devouring sands;
And through all change alone, amazed, apart—
Still, still the same the insatiate human heart.

III.

And Thou, Eternal, Thou art still the same;
  Thou unto whom the first, sad, questioning face
Yearned, for a refuge from the insentient frame
  Of matter that doth grind us; seeking grace
From powers imagined, 'gainst the powers we know;—
  Some charm to avert the whirlwind, bring the tide
And harvest; turn the blind and awful flow
  Of nature! Thou Eternal dost abide

Silent forever, like the unanswering skies
That send but empty echoes to men's cries!

IV.

But not in temples now man's only hope,
  Nor secret ministries of king and priest
Chanting beyond dark gates that never ope
  Unto the people; now no hornèd beast
Looms 'twixt the worshiper and the adored,
  Nor any creature's likeness; He remains
Unknown as erst; yet Him whom we call Lord
  Is worshiped in the fields as in the fanes.
We have but faith; we know not; yet He seems
More near, more human, in our passionate dreams.

V.

We know not, yet the centuries in their course
  Have built an image in the mind of man;
We have but faith, yet that mysterious Force
  Less darkly threatens, looms a friendlier plan.

Far off the singing of the morning stars,
Yet age by age such words of light are spoken
(Like whispered messages through prison bars),
Sometimes men deem the dreadful silence broken,
And hearts that late were famished and afeared
Leap to the Voice and onward fare well cheered.

VI.

Cheered for a little season, but the morrow
Brings the old heartbreak; gone is all the gain;
Though the bowed soul be schooled to its own sorrow,
Ah, heaven! to feel earth's heritage of pain,—
The unescapable anguish of mankind,
That blots out natural joy!—O human soul,
Learn Courage, though the lightning strike thee blind;
Let Duty be thy worship; Love, thy goal:—
Love, Duty, Courage—these make thou thy own,
Till from the unknown we pass into the unknown.

"ANGELO, THOU ART THE MASTER."

I.

ANGELO, thou art the master; for thou in thy art
Compassed the body, the soul; the form and the heart.
Knew where the roots of the spirit are buried and twined,
The springs and the rocks that shall suckle,—and torture and bind.
Large was thy soul like the soul of a god that creates—
Converse it held with the stars and the imminent Fates.
Knewest thou—Art is but Beauty perceived and expressed,
And the pang of that Beauty had entered and melted thy breast.
Here by thy Slave, again, after long years do I bow,—
Angelo, thou art the master, yea, thou, and but thou.

Here is the crown of all beauty that lives in the world;
Spirit and flesh breathing forth from these lips that
are curled
With sweetness and sorrow as never, oh, never before,
And from eyes that are heavy with light, and shall
weep nevermore;
And lo, at the base of the statue, that monster of
shape—
Thorn of the blossom of life, mocking face of the ape.
So cometh morn from the shadow and murk of the
night;
From pain springeth joy, and from flame the keen
beauty of light.

II.

Beauty,—oh, well for the heart that bows down and
adores her:
Heart of mine, hold thou in all the world nothing
before her.
All the fair universe now to her feet that is clinging
Out of the womb of her leaped with the dawn, and
the singing

Of stars. O thou Beautiful! —thee do I worship
and praise
In the dark where thy lamps are; again in thy glory
of days,
Whose end and beginning thou blessest with piercing
delight
Of splendors outspread on the edge of the robe of
the night.

Ah, that sweetness is sent not to him whose dull spirit
would rest
In the bliss of it; no, not the goal, but the passion
and quest;
Not the vale, but the desert. Oh, never soft airs shall
awaken
Thy Soul to the soul of all Beauty, all heaven, and
all wonder;
The summons that comes to thee, mortal, thy spirit
to waken,
Shall be the loud clarion's call and the voices of
thunder.

A WINTER TWILIGHT IN PROVENCE.

A STRANGER in a far and ancient land,
At evening-light I wander. Shade on shade
The mountain valleys darken, and the plain
Grows dim beneath a chill and iron sky.
The trees of peace take the last gray of day—
Day that shone soft on olives, misty-green,
And aisles of wind-forbidding cypresses,
And long, white roads, whitely with plane-trees lined,
And farms content, and happy villages,—
A land that lies close in the very heart
Of history,—and brave, and free, and gay;
In all its song lingering one tone of pain.
  But now the wintry twilight silent falls,
And ghosts of other days stalk the lone fields;
While through yon sunk and immemorial road,
Rock-furrowed, rough, and like a torrent's bed,

Far-stretching into night 'twixt twilight farms,
I see in dream the unhistoried armies pass,
With barbarous banners trailing 'gainst the gloom;
Then, in a thought's flash (centuries consumed),
In this deep path a fierce and refluent wave
Brims the confined and onward-pressing march
With standards slantwise borne; so, to the mind,
The all-conquering eagle northward takes its flight,
And one stern empire widens o'er the world.
There looms the arch of war where once, long gone,
In these still fields, against those thymy slopes,
An alien city reared imperial towers:
See sculptured conqueror, and slave in chains
Mournful a myriad years; and near the arch
The heaven-climbing, templed monument
Embossed with horse and furious warrior!
Millenniums have sped since those grim wars
Here grimly carved, the wonder of the churl,—
The very language dead those warriors cried.
Deepens the dusk, and on the neighboring height
A rock-hewn palace cuts the edge of day
In giant ruin stark against the sky:

Ah, misery! I know its piteous tale
Of armed injustice; monstrous, treacherous force.
Deepens the dusk, and the enormous towers,
Still lording o'er a living city near,
Are lost to sight; but not to thought are lost
A hundred stories of the old-time curse—
War and its ravagings. Deepens the dusk
On westward mountains black with olden crime
And steeped in blood spilled in the blessed name
Of him the Roman soldiers crucified—
The Prince of Peace. Deepens the dusk, and all
The nearer landscape glimmers into dark,
And naught shows clear save yonder wayside cross
Against the lurid west whose dying gleam
Of ghastly sunlight frights the brooding soul.

Dear country mine! far in that viewless west,
And ocean-warded, strife thou too hast known;
But may thy sun hereafter bloodless shine,
And may thy way be onward without wrath,
And upward on no carcass of the slain;
And if thou smitest, let it be for peace

And justice—not in hate, or pride, or lust
Of empire. Mayst thou ever be, O land!
Noble and pure as thou art free and strong:
So shalt thou lift a light for all the world
And for all time, and bring the Age of Peace.

ST.-REMY DE PROVENCE, January, 1896.

II

"THE POET'S DAY."

THE poet's day is different from another,
Though he doth count each man his own heart's brother.
So crystal-clear the air that he looks through,
It gives each color an intenser hue;
Each bush doth burn, and every flower flame;
The stars are sighing; silence breathes a name.
The world wherein he wanders, dreams, and sings
Thrills with the beating of invisible wings;
And all day long he hears from hidden birds
The low, melodious pour of musicked words.

"HOW TO THE SINGER COMES THE SONG?"

I.

How to the singer comes the song?
At times a joy, alone;
A wordless tone
Caught from the crystal gleam of ice-bound trees;
Or from the violet-perfumed breeze;
Or the sharp smell of seas
In sunlight glittering many an emerald mile;
Or the keen memory of a love-lit smile.

II.

Thus to the singer comes the song:
Gazing at crimson skies
Where burns and dies
On day's wide hearth the calm celestial fire,
The poet with a wild desire
Strikes the impassioned lyre,
Takes into tunèd sound the flaming sight
And ushers with new song the ancient night.

III.

How to the singer comes the song?
Bowed down by ill and sorrow
On every morrow,—
The unworded pain breaks forth in heavenly
  singing;
Not all too late dear solace bringing
To broken spirits winging
Through mortal anguish to the unknown rest,—
A lyric balm for every wounded breast.

IV.

How to the singer comes the song?
How to the summer fields
Come flowers? How yields
Darkness to happy dawn? How doth the night
Bring stars? Oh, how do love and light
Leap at the sound and sight
Of her who makes this dark world seem less
  wrong—
Life of his life, and soul of all his song!

"LIKE THE BRIGHT PICTURE."

LIKE the bright picture ere the lamp is lit,
Or silent page whereon keen notes are writ;
So was my love, all vacant, all unsaid,
Ere she the lamp did light, ere she the music read.

REMEMBRANCE OF BEAUTY.

LOVE'S look finds loveliness in all the world:
Ah, who shall say—This, this is loveliest!
Forgetting that pure beauty is impearled
A thousand perfect ways, and none is best.
Sometimes I deem that dawn upon the ocean
Thrills deeper than all else; but, sudden, there,
With serpent gleam and hue, and fixèd motion,
Niagara curves its scimitar in air.
So when I dream of sunset, oft I gaze
Again from Bellosguardo's misty height,
Or memory ends once more one day of days—
Carrara's mountains purpling into night.
There is no loveliest, dear Love, but thee—
Through whom all loveliness I breathe and see.

MUSIC IN SOLITUDE.

I.

In this valley far and lonely
Birds sang only,
And the brook,
And the rain upon the leaves;
And all night long beneath the eaves
(While with soft breathings slept the housèd cattle)
The hivèd bees
Made music like the murmuring seas;
From lichened wall, from many a leafy nook,
The chipmunk sounded shrill his tiny rattle;
Through the warm day boomed low the droning flies,
And the huge mountain shook
With the organ of the skies.

II.

Dear these songs unto my heart;
But the spirit longs for art,
Longs for music that is born
Of the human soul forlorn,
Or the beating heart of pleasure.
Thou, sweet girl, didst bring this boon
Without stint or measure!
Many a tune
From the masters of all time
In my waiting heart made rhyme.

III.

As the rain on parchèd meadows,
As cool shadows
Falling from the sultry sky,
As loved memories die,
But live again when a well-tunèd voice
Makes with old joy the grievèd heart rejoice,
So came once more with thy clear touch

The melodies I love—
Ah, not too much,
But all earth's natural songs far, far above!
For they are nature felt, and living,
And human, and impassioned;
And they full well are fashioned
To bring to sound and sense the eternal striving,
The inner soul of the inexpressive world,
The meaning furled
Deep at the heart of all,—
The thought that mortals name divine,
Whereof all beauty is the sign,
That comes—ah! surely comes—at music's solemn call.

"A POWER THERE IS."

A POWER there is that trembles through the earth;
It lives in nature's mirth,
Making that fearful as the touch of pain;
It strikes the sun-lit plain,
And harvests flash, or bend with rushing rain;
It is not far when tempests make their moan,
And lightnings leap, and falls the thunder-stone.
It comes in morning's beam of living light,
And the imperial night
Knows it and all its company of stars,
And the auroral bars.
Through nature all, the subtile current thrills;
It built in flood and fire the crystal hills;
It molds the flowers,
And all the branchèd forests that abide
Forever on the teeming mountain-side.

It lives where music times the soft, processional hours;
And where on that lone hill of art
Proud Phidias carved in stone his lyric heart;
And where wild battle is, and where
Glad lovers breathe in starry night the quivering air.

THE SONG'S ANSWER.

ME mystic? Have your way!
But sing me, if ye may;—
  Then shall ye know the power
  Of the seed's thought of the flower,
Of the dawn's thought of the day.

THE CELLO.

When late I heard the trembling cello play,
In every face I read sad memories
That from dark, secret chambers where they lay
Rose, and looked forth from melancholy eyes.
So every mournful thought found there a tone
To match despondence; sorrow knew its mate;
Ill fortune sighed, and mute despair made moan;
And one deep chord gave answer, "Late,—too late."
Then ceased the quivering strain, and swift returned
Into its depths the secret of each heart;
Each face took on its mask, where lately burned
A spirit charmed to sight by music's art;
But unto one who caught that inner flame
No face of all can ever seem the same.

THE VALLEY ROAD.

I.

By this road have passed
  Hope and Joy adance;
And one at dark fled fast,—
  Quick breath, and look askance;
And in this dust have dropped
Tears that never stopped.

II.

Childhood, caught by flowers,
  Cannot choose but dally;
Slowly through the hours
  Age creeps down the valley;
Only Youth goes swift—
Eager, and head alift.

III.

Summer, and the night,
  Calm and cloudless moon,—
And lo! a path of light!
  Heaven would come too soon
To lovers wandering slowly
Through the starlight holy.

IV.

And by this road was borne,—
  Betwixt sweet banks of fern,
And willow rows, and corn,—
  He, who will return
Not, though others may,
The old familiar way.

V.

Two streams within these walls
  For ever and ever flow;

Back and forth the current falls,
  The long processions go;
A hundred years have flown,
The human tides pour on,—

VI.

And shall, when you and I
  Pass no more again.
Beneath the bending sky
  Shall be no lack of men;
Never the road run bare,
Though other feet may fare.

HAWTHORNE IN BERKSHIRE.

MOUNTAINS and valleys! dear ye are to me:
  Your streams wild-wandering, ever-tranquil lakes,
  And forests that make murmur like the sea;
  And this keen air that from the hurt soul takes
Its pain and languor:—Doubly dear ye are
  For many a lofty memory that throws
  A splendor on these heights.—'Neath yon low star,
  That like a dewdrop melts in heaven's rose,
Dwelt once a starry spirit; there he smote
  Life from the living hills; a little while
  He rested from the raging of the world.
This Brook of Shadows, whose dark waters purled
  Solace to his deep mind, it felt his smile—
  Haunted, and melancholy, and remote.

LATE SUMMER.

I.

THOUGH summer days are all too fleet,
  Not yet the year is touched with cold;
Through the long billows of the wheat
  The green is lingering in the gold.

II.

The birds that thrilled the April copse,
  Ah! some have flown on silent wings;
Yet one sweet music never stops:
  The constant vireo sings and sings.

AN HOUR IN A STUDIO.

Each picture was a painted memory
Of the far plains he loved, and of their life
Weird, mystical, dark, inarticulate,—
And cities hidden high against the blue,
Whose sky-hung steps one Indian could guard.
The enchanted Mesa there its fated wall
Lifted, and all its story lived again,—
How, in the happy planting time, the strong
Went down to push the seeds into the sand,
Leaving the old and sick. Then reeled the world
And toppled to the plain the perilous path.
Death climbed another way to them who stayed.
He showed us pictured thirst, a dreadful sight;
And many tales he told that might have come,—
Brought by some planet-wanderer,—fresh from Mars,
Or from the silver deserts of the moon.

But I remember better than all else
One night he told of in that land of fright,—

The love-songs swarthy men sang to their herds
On the high plains to keep the beasts in heart;
Piercing the silence one keen tenor voice
Singing "Ai nostri monti" clear and high:
Instead of stakes and fences round about
They circled them with music in the night.

ILLUSION.

WHAT strange, fond trick is this mine eyes are playing!
  I know 't is but the visioning mind perplexes,—
  The inward sight the outer sense betraying,—
  Yet the sweet lie the spirit wounds and vexes:
As at still midnight pondering here, and reading,
  Right on the book's white page, and 'twixt the lines,
  And wreathing through the words, and quick
    receding,
  Only to come again (as 'mid the vines
The dryads flash and hide), white arms are gleaming,
  A light hand hovers, curvèd lips are red,
  Locks in a warm and soundless wind are streaming
Across the image of one glorious head;
  No more,—no more,—shut now the volume lies
  On that swift, piercing look, those haunting eyes.

A SONG OF THE ROAD.

Speed, speed, speed
Through the day, through the night!
Cities are beads on the thread of our flight;
Peaks melt in peaks and are lost in the air.
  Speed, speed, speed,—
    But, oh, the dearth of it—
    Thou not there !

Every journey is good if love be the goal of it.
What 's all the world if love 's not the soul
    of it,—
What were the worth of it—
Thou not there!

"NOT HERE."

I.

NOT here, but somewhere, so men say,
More bright the day,
And the blue sky
More nigh;
Somewhere, afar, the bird of dawn sings sweeter;
Somewhere completer
The round of hopes and heart-beats that make life
More than a bootless strife.

II.

But, ah! there be that know
Where joy alone doth grow.
Led by one true star,
The journey is not far.
'T is in a garden in no distant land,
High-walled on every hand;
And the key thereof
Is love.

"'NO, NO,' SHE SAID."

I.

"No, no," she said;
"I may not wed;
If say I must—*nay* must I say;
I cannot stay;
Nay, nay, I needs must flout thee!"

II.

He turned about;
His life went out;
"If go I must, so must I go!"
Cried she—"No, no;
Ah, what were life without thee!"

A SOUL LOST, AND FOUND.

I.

Lo ! here another
Soul has gone down.
Hope led each morrow;
Honor was all;
Faith had no fall;
Fortune no frown.
Brother by brother
Bowed to each sorrow.
None had lost heart;
Life was love, life was art.

II.

We could but follow !
Quenchless his fire;

The mightier the burden
The stronger his soul,
The higher the goal.
Now see the mire
Soil him and swallow!
Heaven! what guerdon
Worth such a cost!
Love, art, life,—lost, all lost.

III.

Down to the pallid
Figure of death
Love's face is pressing;
Listens and waits,
Beseeching the Fates
For heart-beat and breath—
Sign clear and valid,
Life still confessing.
Dead! He is dead!
All is lost!—He has fled.

IV.

Behold now, a moving,
A flutter of life !
Forth from the starkness,
Horror, and slime,
See, he doth climb.
With himself is the strife;
Back to the loving
From mire and the darkness,
Back to the sun !
He has fought—he has won.

"THIS HOUR MY HEART WENT FORTH, AS IN OLD DAYS."

This hour my heart went forth, as in old days,
To one I loved, forgetting she was dead—
So fluttered back the message, like the dove
That found no rest in all the weltering world.
Is it then so—all blankness and black void,
No welcome, no response, no voice, no sign!
Ah, Heaven! let us be foolish—give us faith
In what is not; cheat us a little longer;
Comfort us mortals with envisioned forms;
Let us, though but in dreams, see spirits near,
And touch the draperies of imagined shapes
That hold the souls we love,—that have gone forth
Into the land of shadows, but still live
In memory, oh, most dear! Beguile our lives
With dim, half-fashioned phantoms of dead hours,
Lest the long way grow hateful;—give us faith
Unreasoned, vague, unsubstanced, but still faith;
For faith is hope, and hope alone is life.

"EVEN WHEN JOY IS NEAR."

Even when joy is near
These ghosts of banished thoughts do haunt the mind:
The awful void of space wherein our earth,
An atom in the unending whirl of stars,
Circles, all helpless, to a nameless doom;
The swift, indifferent marshaling of fate
Whereby the world moves on, rewarding vice
And punishing angelic innocence
As 't were the crime of crimes; the brute, dull, slow
Persistence in the stifled mind of man
Of forces that drive all his being back
Into the slime; the silent cruelty
Of nature, that doth crush the unseen soul
Hidden within its sensitive shell of flesh;
The anguish and the sorrow of all time,—

These are forever with me,—but grow dim
When I remember my sweet mother's face.
Somewhere, at heart of all, the right must reign
If in the garden of the infinite
Such loveliness be brought to perfect bloom.

RESURRECTION.

BACK to my body came I in the gray of the dawning.
Back to my bed in the mold, 'neath the sod and the
blossoms;
Not strange seemed my natural couch, not new, not
afflicting;
But strange now, and new, and afflicting my natural
body,
Alien long while my soul took the wings of the
morning.
I lifted my hands to the light—then swiftly I followed,
With fingers that carefully pressed, the curve of the
muscles;
All was familiar; this was the frame I had nurtured,
I had loved as a man loves the body so long his
companion;
Again was I 'ware of the brow where the dew of
sweet kisses

Fell, ere forth went the stripling to life and the shudder
Of battle;—again from the mirror of waters the features
Not unloved of dear comrades looked forth. I beheld in amazement
The bodily presence so long laid aside and forgotten;
Overwhelmed was my soul with its shackles; I grieved, I lamented
As a prisoner dragged back to his cell, as an eagle recaptured.

"AS SOARS THE EAGLE."

As soars the eagle, intimate of light,
Fear not the face of the sun;
Nor all the blasts of earth.
Child of Him, the untrembling One,
Oh, prove thee worthy of thy birth!

Let no ill betray thee!
Let no death dismay thee!

The eagle seeks the sky,
Nor fears the infinite light;
Thus, soul of mine, escape the night
And 'gainst the morning fly!

III

ROBERT GOULD SHAW.

(THE MONUMENT BY AUGUSTUS ST. GAUDENS.)

I.

FIXED in one desire,
  Thrilled by one fierce fire,
Marching men and horse,
And he the youthful rider—one soul, one aim,
  one force.

II.

Onward he doth press;
Moving, but motionless;
Resolute, intent,—
As on some mighty errand the willing youth
  were bent.

III.

Onward, though he hears
Father's, sisters' tears;

Onward, though before him
—Grief more near, more dear—the breaking
heart that bore him.

IV.

Onward, though he leaves
One who lonely grieves;
Oh, keep him, Fate! from harm,
For on his dewy lips the bridal kiss is warm.

V.

What doth he behold
Making the boy so bold?
Speak with whispering breath!
O Fate, O Fame, O radiant soul in love with
glorious Death!

VI.

Eyes that forward peer—
Why have they no fear?

Because, through blood and blight,
They see the golden morning burst and bring
the living light;

VII.

See War the fetters strike
From white and black alike;
See, past the pain and scorn,
A nation saved, a race redeemed, and freedom
newly born;

VIII.

See, in days to come,—
When silent War's loud drum,
Ere civic wrong shall cease,—
Heroes as pure and brave arise on battle-fields
of peace.

"THE NORTH STAR DRAWS THE HERO."

(TO H. N. G.)

THE North Star draws the hero; he abides
  Steadfast though death defends the unending quest.
But, ah, more faithful still the love that hides
  In woman's empty arms and aching breast!

GLAVE.

This day I read in the sad scholar's page
  That the old earth is withered and undone;
  That faith and great emprise beneath the sun
  Are vain and empty in our doting age;
'T were best to calm the spirit's noble rage,
  To live in dreams, and all high passion shun,
  While round and round the aimless seasons run,—
  Pleasured alone with dead art's heritage.
Then, as I read, outshone thy face of youth,
  Hero and martyr of humanity,
  Dead yesterday on Afric's shore of doom!
Ah, no; Faith, Courage fail not, while lives Truth,
  While Pity lives, while man for man can die,
  And deeds of glory light the dark world's gloom.

OF HENRY GEORGE,

WHO DIED FIGHTING AGAINST POLITICAL TYRANNY AND CORRUPTION.

Now is the city great! That deep-voiced bell
  Tolls for a martyred hero. Such is he
Who loved her, strove for her, and nobly fell.
  His fire be ours,—the passion to be free.

NEW YORK, 1897.

SCORN.

Who are the men that good men most despise ?
  Not they who, ill begot and spawned in shame,
  Riot and rob, or rot before men's eyes,—
  Who basely live, and dying leave no name.
These are the piteous refuse of mankind,
  Fatal the ascendant star when they were born,—
  Distort in body, starved in soul and mind;
  Ah, not for them the good man's bitter scorn !
He, only, is the despicable one
  Who lightly sells his honor as a shield
  For fawning knaves, to hide them from the sun;—
Too nice for crime, yet, coward, he doth yield
  For crime a shelter. Swift to Paradise
  The contrite thief, not Judas with his price !

THE HEROIC AGE.

He speaks not well who doth his time deplore,
Naming it new and little and obscure,
Ignoble and unfit for lofty deeds.
All times were modern in the time of them,
And this no more than others. Do thy part
Here in the living day, as did the great
Who made old days immortal! So shall men,
Gazing long back to this far-looming hour,
Say: "Then the time when men were truly men:
Though wars grew less, their spirits met the test
Of new conditions; conquering civic wrong;
Saving the state anew by virtuous lives;
Guarding the country's honor as their own,
And their own as their country's and their sons':
Defying leaguèd fraud with single truth;
Not fearing loss; and daring to be pure.

When error through the land raged like a pest,
They calmed the madness caught from mind to mind
By wisdom drawn from eld, and counsel sane;
And as the martyrs of the ancient world
Gave Death for man, so nobly gave they Life:
Those the great days, and that the heroic age."

ATHENS, 1896.

THE SWORD OF THE SPIRIT.

(IN MEMORY OF JOE EVANS.)

Too much of praise for the quick, pitiless blow!
Justice doth lean on strength, full well we know;
But the sharp, glittering sword that strikes for right
Takes fame too easily. Thank Heaven for might,
Which is Heaven's servant, oft! Yet he 's not man
Who, when the heart 's afire, no brave deed can.
Praise thou the clenched fist that, when blood is hot,
On itself tightens, but descendeth not.
Aye, praise the sword undrawn, the bolt unsped,
The rage suppressed till the true word is said.
Might of the spirit, this shalt thou extol,
And holy weakness of the conquering soul.

And on this day, when one well loved has passed
From suffering to the unknown peace, at last,
Would I might praise, as nobly as I ought,
The hero-soldier who no battle fought,—
Or, rather, one who, facing fate's worst frown,
The spirit's sword but with his life laid down.

The soul that from that body, bent and frail,
Peered out, did at no earthly terror quail.
To face an army he was brave enough;
Martyrs and conquerors are of that stuff.
And in the civic conflict that was waged
Year after year, his knightly spirit raged;
He could not bear his country should have blame,
So this slight warrior did the mighty shame.
Yet Beauty was his passion, and the art
To paint it—that it might not all depart.
He loved the gentlest things; there was a grace
In his sad look surpassing many a face
More beautiful. Ah, back, ye bitter tears!
He, lover of light and gladness, all these years
Fighting twin demons of keen pain and doom;
He, of such humor that the very tomb
Might snatch a brightness from his presence there!
But no; not bright the tomb. We, in despair,
Seek through the world again a charm like this—
That which our friend has taken we shall forever miss.

April, 1898.

"THROUGH ALL THE CUNNING AGES."

I.

THROUGH all the cunning ages
  Mankind hath made for man
From out his loves and rages
  A god to bless and ban.

II.

When he his foe despises
  This god he calls to curse;
And would he win earth's prizes
  His praise doth man rehearse.

III.

So, when he craves the guerdon
  Of others' land and pelf,
He flings the blame and burden
  On this shadow of himself.

IV.

If, spite of all their ranting,
  There reigns a God indeed,
How well he hates the canting
  That framed their sordid creed!

V.

"Lay not to me your hollow
  And broken words of faith,—
To sin that good may follow
  No law of mine," he saith.

VI.

"If, 'twixt your tribes and nations.
  There lives no law but might,
Not myriad incantations
  Can make your evil right.

VII.

"Ye call me 'God of battle';
  I weary while ye slay.
Are ye my hornèd cattle
  To find no better way?"

ONE COUNTRY—ONE SACRIFICE.

(ENSIGN WORTH BAGLEY, MAY 11, 1898.)

IN one rich drop of blood, ah, what a sea
  Of healing! Thou, sweet boy, wert first to fall
  In our new war; and thou wert southron all!
There is no North, no South,—remembering thee.

"WHEN WITH THEIR COUNTRY'S ANGER."

I.

WHEN with their country's anger
  They flame into the fight,—
On sea, in treacherous forest,
  To strike with main and might,—

II.

He shows the gentlest mercy
  Who rains the deadliest blows;
Then quick war's hell is ended,
  And home the hero goes.

III.

What stays the noblest memory
  For all his years to keep?
Not of the foemen slaughtered,
  But rescued from the deep!

IV.

Rescued with peerless daring!
  Oh, none shall forget that sight,
When the unaimed cannon thundered
  In the ghastly after-fight.

V.

And, now, in the breast of the hero
  There blooms a strange, new flower,
A blood-red, fragrant blossom
  Sown in the battle-hour.

VI.

'T is not the Love of Comrades,—
  That flower forever blows,—
But the brave man's Love of Courage,
  The Love of Comrade-Foes.

VII.

For since the beginning of battles
  On the land and on the wave,
Heroes have answered to heroes,
  The brave have honored the brave.

1898.

A VISION.

ALL round tne glimmering circuit of the isle
Audibly pulsed the ocean. In the dark
Of the thick wood a voice not of its own
Might come to sharpened ears; a sound suppressed,—
The rustling of an armèd multitude
Who toss in sleep, or, wakening, watch for death.
Beneath the tropic stars that in strange skies
Drew close and glittered large, I saw in dream
A Soul pass hoveringly.
                                        Then came I near
And questioned of that Ghost, who answer made
Like a deep, murmuring wind that slowly draws
Through dim memorial aisles of ancient time:

"I am the mother of men, and from my womb
Came all the dead and living. I am cursed
With memory, with knowledge of what is,
And what shall be; yet, verily, am I blessed

With these three knowledges,—my children I
Have seen these myriad years grow, age by age,
More wise, more just, more joyous, yet have I
Seen mutual slaughter sow the earth with tears.
In this New World here had I hoped my children
Would learn to unlearn the path mankind has climbed
Over its slain to happiness and power;
For soon or late I know that boon shall come,
And in the wars of peace the race shall wax
Manlier, purer, gentler, and more wise.
But now again the sacred truce is broken,
And bleeds this breast at every wound and sigh,
And aches my mother-heart with the new pain
Of mortal mothers comfortless forever."

Then passed the Spirit from my dream at dawn;
I woke into another day of war
With news of splendid deeds, and victory,—
Yet still I heard that brooding shade lament.

1898.

THE WORD OF THE WHITE TSAR.

THIS day, a strange and beautiful word was spoken,—
Not with the voice of a child, nor the voice of a
woman,
Nor yet with the voice of a poet, the melody
sounded,—
Forth from the lips of a warrior, girt for the battle,
Breathed this word of words o'er a world astonished.

Prisoners returning from war, and conquering armies,
Navies flushed with new and amazing victory,
Heard the message, so strange, so high, so entrancing,
And soldiers dying of wounds or the wasting of fever.
In tropic islands it sounded, through wrecks of cities;
O'er burning plains where warlike death was in
waiting;

Armies and navies confronting, in watchful silence,
Heard it and wondered; statesmen stopped their debates,
And turning their eyes toward the voice, with its meaning unlooked for,
Listened and smiled with the smile and the sneer of the cynic.
But the mothers of youths who had died of their wounds and of fever,
And the poor crushed down by the price of the glory of battle
And the weight of the wars that have been, and that yet are preparing,
They from their burdens looked up and uttered their blessing:
For Peace—the Peace of God—was the warrior's prayer!

And I, who heard, I saw in a waking vision
An image familiar long to the hearts of mortals,—
A face of trouble, a brow celestial, yet human,—
In a dream of the day, I saw that suffering spirit,

Him accustomed to labor, to anguish not alien,
Still mourning for men alone in the valley of
shadows ; —
I dreamed that he lifted that face of infinite sorrow,
And harkened,—when lo! a light in those eyes of
sadness
Came sudden as day that breaks from the mountains
of Moab.

IV

A SONG FOR DOROTHEA, ACROSS THE SEA.

I.

A SONG for you, my darling,
  For your own, dear, only sake.
You bid me sing,—so does the spring
  Bid the birds awake,
  And quick with molten music the dewy branches
      quake.

II.

A song for you, my darling,
  To follow you all the day;
And in sweet sleep the song shall keep
  Singing along the way,
  Through dreamland's silver meadows with golden
      lilies gay.

III.

A song for you, my darling,
  For those deep and darkling eyes,
That steadfast shine as the stars divine
  Bright in the midnight skies,
  When the winds blow the clouds from heaven, and
      we gaze with a glad surprise.

IV.

A song for you, my darling,
  A song for that faithful heart
That as true abides as the throbbing tides,
  Though half a world apart—
  So far away is the girl I sing, with only a lover's art.

A BLIND POET.

CALL him not blind
Whose keen, anointed sight,
Pierced every secret of the heart, the mind,
The day, the night.

ON A WOMAN SEEN UPON THE STAGE.

("TESS," AS PLAYED BY MRS. FISKE.)

ALAS, poor, fated, passionate, shivering thing!
So through brief life some dagger-haunted king
Wears a bright sorrow. Thus her life rehearse:
She was a woman; this her crown, her curse.

OF ONE WHO NEITHER SEES NOR HEARS.

(HELEN KELLER.)

I.

SHE lives in light, not shadow;
  Not silence, but the sound
Which thrills the stars of heaven
  And trembles from the ground.

II.

She breathes a finer ether,
  Beholds a keener sun;
In her supernal being
  Music and light are one.

III.

Unknown the subtile senses
  That lead her through the day;

Love, light, and song and color
  Come by another way.

IV.

Sight brings she to the seeing,
  New song to those that hear;
Her braver spirit sounding
  Where mortals fail and fear.

V.

She at the heart of being
  Serene and glad doth dwell;
Spirit with scarce a veil of flesh;
  A soul made visible.

VI.

Or is it only a lovely girl
  With flowers at her maiden breast?
—Helen, here is a book of song
  From the poet who loves you best.

FOR THE ESPOUSALS OF JEANNE ROUMANILLE, OF AVIGNON.

I.

WHILE joy-bells are ringing
  And the high Fates meet thee,
Child of the South, and of singing,
  Singing I greet thee

II.

In thy chaplet one flower
  From a far world!—Wilt wear it?
Rich though thy land, and this hour,
  Thou mayst not forbear it;

III.

Thou wilt welcome and win it;
  It will breathe on, caress thee;
For the fame of thy father is in it;
  His lover doth bless thee!

IV.

His lover—the lover of thee, O Provence;
  Thy blue skies, thy gray mountains;
The heart-beat of Freedom and France
  Shakes thy rivers and fountains,

V.

And makes thee a dream and a passion
  In the souls of all poets forever,—
While from thy fire thou dost fashion
  Beauty and music and art that shall perish, oh,
      never !

TO MARIE JOSEPHINE GIRARD, QUEEN OF THE FÉLIBRES,

ON HER WEDDING-DAY.

QUEENS have there been of many a fair domain
  Of arts, of hearts, of lands.
  Thy sovereignty a threefold realm commands
Who o'er Provence, and Poetry, and Love dost reign.

INSCRIPTION FOR A TOWER IN FLORENCE.

(WRITTEN FOR THE CHATELAINE.)

I.

FOUR-WALLED is my tower:
The first wall is for the dawn that comes from Vallombrosa,
The second wall is for the day that fills with soft fire the green vase of Tuscany,
The third is for the evening twilight that darkens from the Valley of the Arno,
The fourth is for the night and the stars of night.

II.

Four-walled is my tower:
One wall is for the South and the sun,
One is for the West and for memory,
One is for the North and the star that never sets,
And one is for the East and a faith that fares beyond the stars.

III.

Four-walled is my tower:
One wall is for the Spring and for Hope,
One is for Summer and for Love,
One is for Autumn and the Harvest,
One is for Winter and for Waiting.

IV.

Four-walled is my tower:
One is for Childhood and the Innocence of Life,
The second is for Youth and the Joy of Life,
The third is for Manhood and the Fullness of Life,
The fourth is for Old Age and the Wisdom of Life.

V.

Four-walled is my tower:
A Rock for Strength,
A Height for Seeing,
A Beacon for the Stranger,
And a Hearth for Friendship.
Four-walled is my tower
On the Hill of Bellosguardo.

WITH A VOLUME OF DANTE.

O THOU whom Virgil and thy Beatrice
Through life and death, Hell, Purgatory, Heaven,
Led upward into unimagined light,—
Lead thou this soul the way thou, too, didst go
Unto the Light that lights the eternal stars!

www.ingramcontent.com/pod-product-compliance
Lightning Source LLC
LaVergne TN
LVHW021429110826
845150LV00007B/2144

* 9 7 8 1 4 2 5 5 0 6 9 8 8 *